Art you can eat

When we have a fun event, it can be two times the fun with cake. Cakes can be art!

Cake artists do a lot of work to make their cakes look good. They use tools to help them.

Some cakes are made to tower above us. Cake artists have some tricks to help a cake stand tall. Pillars can help to hold it up. Rods can be placed inside.

rods

Some artists use tools to
shape icing. They must
touch the icing gently
so it will not dent.

Powders can tint the icing in different shades.

A spray gun is another good tool because it can spray the cake without touching it.

Spraying over and over
makes this fur look real.

Some artists use piping bags. They take a lot of time to make the piping neat.

When it is done, the piping can make some stunning patterns.

Cake artists start by drawing plans. It can take months of planning until they are done.

Some cakes have hundreds
of small details to add – like
flowers and fruit.

Cake artists make fun cakes too. Some look like real-life things.

Some look like toys.

Others look like books
we might read.

There is nothing a cake artist cannot make with cake!

Words to blend

another	months	others
nothing	some	above
done	touch	touching
stunning	icing	patterns
flowers	pillars	towers
powders	artist	event

Before reading

Synopsis: Take a look at how artists create stunning works of art out of cake.

Review phonemes and graphemes: /ear/ ere, eer; /air/ are, ear, ere; /j/ ge, dge, g; /s/ c, ce, sc, se, st; /c/ ch

Focus phoneme: /u/ **Focus graphemes:** o, o-e, ou

Book discussion: Look at the cover, and read the title together. Ask: *What kind of book do you think this is – fiction or non-fiction? How do you know? What do you think we'll learn in this book?* Talk about cake decorating – what do children already know about this? Share their ideas.

Link to prior learning: Remind children that the sound /u/ as in 'mud' can also be spelled 'o', 'o-e' and 'ou'. Flip through the book and ask children to point out a word with each spelling of the /u/ sound (e.g. some, touch, another).

Vocabulary check: tint: colour – e.g. 'Powders can tint the icing in different shades' means 'Powders can colour the icing in different shades'.

Decoding practice: Display the words 'some', 'another', 'touch' and 'done'. Can children circle the letter string that makes the /u/ sound, and read each word?

Tricky word practice: Display the word 'because'. Explain that the letters 'au' together make the /o/ sound. Practise reading and writing this word.

After reading

Apply learning: Discuss the book. Ask: *Did the cake art in the book look good? Would you want to try doing cake art? Why or why not?*

Comprehension

- What do cake artists use to spray cakes? (a spray gun)
- What can be placed inside a cake to keep it standing up? (rods)
- Is cake art made quickly? (No, it can take months of planning.)

Fluency

- Pick a page that most of the group read quite easily. Ask them to reread it with pace and expression. Model how to do this if necessary.
- Challenge children to read page 16 with plenty of enthusiasm and expression. Remind them to pay attention to the exclamation mark.
- Practise reading the words on page 17.

Tricky words review

have	two	because
ask	of	their
to	are	the
doing	any	laugh
what	people	want